# Reading Lessons

*poems by*

# Mary Fox

*Finishing Line Press*
Georgetown, Kentucky

# Reading Lessons

Copyright © 2019 by Mary Fox
ISBN 978-1-63534-992-4 First Edition
All rights reserved under International and Pan-American Copyright Conventions. No part of this book may be reproduced in any manner whatsoever without written permission from the publisher, except in the case of brief quotations embodied in critical articles and reviews.

## ACKNOWLEDGMENTS

"Empty Air." *Promptly Speaking, a Writing at the Ledges Anthology*, Dragonfly Press, 2018

Special thanks to Rosalie Sanara Petrouske for her editing advice and lovely photography.

Publisher: Leah Maines
Editor: Christen Kincaid
Cover Art: Rosalie Sanara Petrouske
Author Photo: Rosalie Sanara Petrouske
Cover Design: Elizabeth Maines McCleavy

Printed in the USA on acid-free paper.
Order online: www.finishinglinepress.com
also available on amazon.com

Author inquiries and mail orders:
Finishing Line Press
P. O. Box 1626
Georgetown, Kentucky 40324
U. S. A.

# Table of Contents

First Read ........................................................................................... 1

Illegible .............................................................................................. 2

Not Unread, to Uncle Garland who died young ........................ 4

Reading the Score, an oral reading poem ................................... 5

Elizabeth Little Library, an oral reading poem .......................... 7

Street Map Legend: Warren, Michigan ....................................... 9

Reo Town Roll, local address ..................................................... 10

Written Complaints: Rasp, Crackle, Pop, an oral reading poem ...... 11

Body Language ............................................................................ 13

Eastside Hum, street song ........................................................... 14

Palm Read ..................................................................................... 15

Dispensation ................................................................................. 16

Small Print .................................................................................... 17

Girl-praisal ................................................................................... 18

Bible Reading or why I never did well at Trinity Lutheran
    Church Sunday School ........................................................... 19

Ghostwritten ................................................................................ 22

Divorce Decree ............................................................................ 23

Reflective Reading ....................................................................... 24

Love Letters ................................................................................. 25

Unfinished Story ......................................................................... 26

Lip-read ........................................................................................ 27

In Memoriam: Christmas Greetings ......................................... 28

Empty Air ..................................................................................... 29

*I am dedicating this book to friends and family,
who put up with their crazy sister-in-law/sister/aunt/stepmom/pal
and don't cringe when I write about them,
and my writing groups who give me good advice.*

## First Read

She pools beyond my newborn eyes,
an uncertain swimmer treading water
in the churning waves before me.
We've just met, toed the water and stepped in,
just felt the sharpness of the rocky bottom,
just felt the pull of its current.
We haven't found our footing,
and neither of us wants to drown,
and so we float at the mercy of the tide.

Still, I want to trust her
and the strength of her tread—
I want to lean into her cradled arms—
but I've read the quiver in her tongue
and the brine of her eyes,
and I know she is just as scared as I am.
Wearied, she wants me to just stop crying
and vomiting and fall asleep—
because she is tired and overwhelmed.
We both long to fall back
into some safe cave of slumber
where hopes become dreams
and dreams become true.

But then, I'm no baby doll,
and she's on her own,
and nobody is here
to help her pretend,
and when we awaken again,
we'll be neck deep
and still want perfect.

**Illegible**

I see you still, bent over a crossword
inking in sure answers—puzzling the rest
until all the squares fill.
You always found the answers,
but how do I fill in the blanks?
I've pulled your war records,
filled in what I know from growing up
and hearing your jokes
about holding women's breasts
as you gave X-rays.
I imagine your life much darker
than a joke after a beer,
as you escorted wounded from England,
comforting them in a ship's rolling sadness.

Often, I remember you reading mysteries—
I brought them home from our local library.
Nose buried in Sam Spade and Gardner,
you always figured out the plot
long before the book ended.
But how do I solve the mystery of you?
I've grabbed your lineage
the story of your people,
the immigrants scrabbling for life
in Ireland, Indiana, Pennsylvania, Michigan.
I see your school-boy picture.
I look for you in it and find you missing.
I ponder your family:
How did your brother really die?
Who were those cousins we visited at reunions?
Here and there, I guess a word or two
of the pages you presented me.

In moments, I still see you, riding beside me
to a Red Wings game
giving my sixteen-year-old ears directions.
Even back then, I wondered
why you refused to drive.
I remember sitting at a game,
when a puck flew.
The glass crumbled before us.
I wondered why I could never
shatter that glass between us.
Now, long dead you slide away:
your image dissolves like safety glass,
and you are buried in crumbling mementoes
blurred by time. I cannot fathom
where my father lies in them.
I want to find you,
but you are gone on the page—
lost under illegible scrawls,
unreadable.

## Not Unread:  To Uncle Garland who died young

Do not think because your life was short
you were unread.  My child's eyes read
you on a summer's day
when you stood me on your new red Olds.
Mother admonished you to "get me off "
before I "scratched the paint."
You laughed
then balanced two-year-old legs
on a fender slick with wax.

I was only five that day you died.
I remember the sprint
and the cold scramble
up a neighbor's heating oil tank
waiting for another kind of winter.
Only Mother could coax me down.

I am old now, much older than you.
Still, I read your letters from France and Germany.
A gunner and a sometimes cook—
I remember my mother used your recipes
and taught me your wisdom of salt.
Every day I see you with Mother,
your wife, and Grandfather standing in pictures
I hang in my hall—
You were someone I needed to know,
if only briefly—
reassurance even then
someone loved me as I was: imperfect,
off-balance and not quite formed.

## Reading the Score, an oral reading poem

My mother, a prim angel in church clothes,
sat a pew, lucid and prepared.
Gazing on her was a revelation in itself—
until the organ sounded.
Then she lost some of her celestial qualities.
Her voice was not just off-key.
It was a discordant, cringe-worthy mess.
I sang next to her in a voice so small
I was nearly silent.
I knew early as much as I loved a song,
my notes were off,
and my pitch just as nasally,
and my singing voice just as grating
as my mother's.

Still, as I grew, I knew
as my mother's voice croaked out the words,
the melody put joy in her heart.
She never ignored a song she loved,
and so she taught me to sing beyond my handicap
to the soul of the music
and the joy of the music itself.
Now whenever music plays,
it is her voice I miss.
And so I, too, sing louder than I should
in my tuneless voice and find
the love of music in my tapping toes.

I tell you, my loves, that you, too,
must read the music.
All around you people listen,
and you must sing what you love.
You know the notes,
though they might as yet
perch unsyllabled on your tongue.

Even if your throat croaks the lines,
drums call you, so before the melody escapes,
and you lose the beat in a fading heart,
sing!
You were born with scores—
gifted on your first day
with tunes all your own.
Sing so that other hearts
will hear the bravery, the truth,
the kindness upon your lips.
Open the hymnal of your heart,
and sing its music.

## Elizabeth Little Library: an oral reading poem

Elizabeth Little Elementary School had a small room
turned library off the back-stage door,
in the auditorium slash gym slash cafeteria.
There teachers housed a set of robin-egg blue books
titled with the name of every famous American
since the pilgrim dawn.
I read every one.
And it was on those books' cream-colored pages
my rebellion began at age six
in Warren, Michigan, where I grew up
shaded by trees rooted in racism and slavery,
planted where redlined Detroit
met Southerners settling in boxed-house suburbs,
near enough to factories to work
and far enough not to smell the stink.

So when my Kentucky-born mother
told me black people were not smart
because their skull bones were so thick,
they didn't leave room for brains,
I already knew, that George Washington Carver's research
had invented my favorite lunch—peanut butter and jelly;
Frederick Douglass led an anti-slavery movement
and had more education than my mama,
daddy, and grand-daddies combined;
and Harriet Tubman smuggled people
out of slavery into Canada via Michigan.

And because I loved my daddy, who brought me home,
nearly every day, three newspapers that I read to imitate him
then did the easy crosswords while he did the hard ones,
I sat on his lap to watch Walter Cronkite.
So I already knew who Gandhi was and Martin Luther King
and had watched some black school children walk
protected by Eisenhower's gauntlet
into a Little Rock Schoolhouse.

So when my mother preached ignorance
I pointed out black people were trying to get into school
to not be so ignorant and that my *Weekly Reader* SAID
that thick skulls were a scientific myth.

Now my mother was not a woman
easily swayed from her beliefs.
Still, sixty some years later, I believe I succeeded.
One day I walked into her assisted-living facility
and joined her in the bar area
where the residents did happy hour on Fridays
between two and four, snacking and sipping Bailey's over ice.
She wanted to introduce me to her best friend
Doris, a retired black school teacher.

Now the point of my story is this.
I did not change my mother's perspective in a day
nor without the help of other people.
However, nothing works like the persistence of truth.
And whether you are six or sixty
you must witness that truth,
for that truth to drown out the lies.
Nothing wears on stone like the drip of water,
and nothing cuts through
when someone waxes over the truth
like a little friction and a little heat.
And though, some may equivocate, distort,
and flat-out fabricate,
every heart has a truth-detector
that it cannot deny,
and you can awaken it with a child's breath
or an old lady's Tuesday evening poem
at the Robin Theatre,
and change the hearts around you.

## Street Map Legend: Warren, Michigan

When the city paved our neighborhood,
we stepped off the curbs
fronting our postwar houses,
wedged between pre-war Cape Cods
and leftover farmhouses, to street-dance
our celebration of the cemented progress
of sidewalks and mudless roads.
Mostly, though, we mapped out
our weeks, by the migration of men.
Absent from our households
most days as they worked the odd shifts
of factories, they reappeared weekends
to fenced backyards and brick patios.
They set aluminum chairs arcing
charcoal grills they lit early to cook on.
After, they drank Pabst Blue Ribbon
then listened to Tigers
blare through open windows.
Work-weary in webbed chairs,
those men leaned back,
hidden by their unattached garages,
as they ignored the sheds at fence lines.
Push-mowers and garden tools
waited for Sunday evening labor.
Spring to late summer,
they minded twilight children
running bikes and scooters up long driveways,
playing the whole block,
till streetlamps called them home.
Here men forgot the sharp din of picket
or assembly lines and muted
the echoes of battlefields.
They curved their backbones and let beer
and Friday night barbecue solace them
as giggles and Van Patrick serenaded them
in the flicker of fireflies
dancing on brick.

## Reo Town Roll, local address

Reo Town's rolled out the welcome mat
since Frenchie's bar sold lunch tacos
to coeds with warnings on the green sauce
and coming solo to a night-time crowd.
Even then, it sparked its own glory—
spinning fender-boned
and axle-geared trucks from its lines.
It still cranks that creator's rhythm:
it's a poet's meter, a songster's lilt,
a dreamer's hammer, a chef's spoon,
a new line rolling
to set feet to tappin',
lips to smackin', hearts to carin',
minds to thinkin'.
It fires us up and welds us together.
We drive forward, onward,
upward rising, on new-rolled streets,
still gunning REO's engines
into tomorrow.

## Written Complaints: Rasp, Crackle, Pop, an oral reading poem

**Rasp**
Complaints rasp like dry cornstalks in winter's wind.
Their whispery murmurs gust in,
even before I've identified syllables of discontent.
How do I mouth words, painful knowings,
that sound like some sci-fi fraud?
My planet *is* dying.  Japan *leaks* radiation
into oceans already *choking* on Nestle plastic
that drains Michigan's watersheds even as Line 5 oil
*threatens* the Great Lakes.
Oil and coal *boil* the planet.

**Crackle**
Grievances crack hearts and hopes,
sinking us into those dark rivers—
where the faithless floes of groundless belief
chunk and dam our progress
then threaten our existence.
Our faces etch in despair.
How do I give voice
when my impotence wars
with my weaponless arms?
No bullet rewinds the clock,
nor silences the lips of avarice.
What undoes delay?
Chances tick away, then pass return.
Who re-writes science reports?
Excises forbidden words, erasing
the possibility of change?
We break on the emptiness of our courage.

**Pop**
We must pop the bubbles of lies.
Let the ground implode like sinkholes,
and collapse on the emptiness of promises.
When I press the weight of reality,
can I explode the falsehoods, like volcanic heat rising?
Void our oozing pimples festering deep
in the halls of government?
Drain, remove, uproot, restore—
Every moment lost, scars deepen.
Can we rattle certitude?
Stop murder for profit?

**Rasp, Crackle, Pop**
Or do we just feed the din
with more: rasp, crackle, pop?

**Body Language**


She's disappearing—
swallowing air and nicotine
instead of food,
hoping just to breathe enough—
inhale enough smoke—
to haze the fears.
It's not just today's torment
that compresses her lips
to seal her tongue from food.
It's the memory—
>	husband *weeping* with pain
>	unable to sleep, legs crushed,
>	misshapen by the cruelty of metal and alcohol.
>	hungry children cry
>	and she cannot not work
>	because her husband weeps
>	unable to walk, bedridden.
>	house disappearing
>	under unpaid bills. . .
And **right now** seems far away.
because **yesterday** looms—
just when they've recovered
just when she's grown unafraid.
So she slips into her size zero
and heads to work
while he lies
alone
in a hospital
waiting for test results
again.

Weighted by more than the trays
she carries, she works until her shift ends
then smokes a cigarette
to fill an empty space inside
before she pushes through
to what awaits her
beyond the doors.

**Eastside Hum, street song**

Once, under an April moon,
I sat a lover's bed in Eastside
and gazed down to Michigan Ave.
The street buzzed
through that paned window,
as my lover wrapped arms around me.
Whenever I walk down Eastside
I still feel that current vibrate:
It hums at Everybody Reads
if I stop to buy a poet's book—
at a goddess's tarot read—
at the Green Door
when a Wednesday-wail
blues tune sifts to the street.
I hear it sitting in Dagwood's—
where once I held that lover's hand—
in a poured beer's bubble-bursts
as burgers sizzle
on a home-game Saturday.
I still enjoy that purr—
still remember that deliciousness
of a lover's lips above the streetlamps
under an April moon
on Eastside.

**Palm Read**

A splayed palm flashes garish pink
above the side-street door I push through.
Inside, a black tablecloth ripples its fringe
in greeting.  On a table top, Cheiro's book lies
open to "Mounts." Then through an arch,
the reader slides to gesture a chair.
Prices set, she traces the swirls
on my lamp-lit fingertips
and maps creases in my tingling palms.
I turn toward the gloom
of a twilight window,
entranced to wonder by lights
twinkling like stars,
dancing in a darkening sky:

> Was my fate written in stars?
> Trapped in a sun's fading rays?
> Was it energized by swirling comets
> and space debris making rounds?
>
> Was it charted in the rotation of planets?
> Beamed down on the moon's light
> from a dark side on a cool winter morn?
>
> Was it black-holed in the dimness of swallowing suns?
> Was it written on a molecule of time?
>
> Or could I just grasp it in the palm of my hand?

## Dispensation

You probably would not like
that I wear a ring
my first husband gave me.
I just sized it again—
an engagement ring
he surprised me with—
and I was lost in
a swirl of stony glitter,
a first-love whirlwind
as I whispered, "yes."

Back then I didn't even know to what.

Instead, you gave me flowers.
They poise around my deck
still blooming and swelling in the sun.
Clumped with bees and hornets
drawn to the sweetness,
the rich savory sap,
they burst into hum of love
every summer day.

I guess I forgive you
for dying too young.

## Small Print

The hospital looms dizzily above her,
but she carries precious cargo—
a child of light and stars
who careens forward, arms open,
and sparks her day.
So when she tumbles from the car
and stumbles with him into the waiting room
she's already signed in.
No one read her the contract
when she was 19 and pregnant
and enlisted into parenthood,
and she knows now nothing
she signs will cost as much.

Even here, no one mentions the small print
that runs through PIC lines
into her baby's arms and legs.
Certainly, nobody read her the part
where his well-being is beyond her control—
the part where other people's carelessness
or lies or thoughtlessness or addictions
threaten him.
And though the safety nest
she and his father have built for him
sits waiting, no one highlighted
the part about how nothing they do
will be enough.

So she sits humbled as they fill him with tubes,
and she doesn't cry
because someone has to stay sane.
She holds his hand then smooths
his cheeks damp with sweat, and prays
for good news in the fine print
of the morning report.

## Girl-praisal

I stand waiting for the lifeguard to signal
when we can enter the pool,
and the guy with the lisp
stands next to me giving me
girl-praisal—
that neck to ankle eye-sweep
that sets my value at his interest.

Never mind that I am smart
and funny, well-traveled and more,
my worth is set between chin and ankle
weighed on his visual scale.

And never mind that his belly bulges
and his eyes bead,
and he hasn't so far said anything
I'm vaguely interested in.
Weighed in the commerce of relationship
what matters to him is his desire and preference.
My worth?  Just a commodity
assessed in one girl-praisal
two-second sweep.

## Bible Reading or why I never did well at Trinity Lutheran Church Sunday School

*Eve's Apples:*
If God put a tree full of sweet apples
to tempt *me* into reason
and fill *me* with knowledge,
I would have not just taken a bite,
I'd have chewed that tree bare,
savoring each mouthful,
and leaving the sad, seedless cores for Adam.
I'd swallow all the seeds,
and with all that knowledge inside me,
I'd hope to sprout a truth.

*Adam's first wife:*
Like Lilith, I'll never be servant
to someone created equal to me,
but too lazy to find out all he can
about the world he lives in.
I don't care if some Adams calls me a demon
and spreads rumors of my dangers to the world.
Anytime someone tries to gaslight me
about what it means to be good and decent,
telling me I must be obedient and bendable,
I let out a howl, raise my hackles,
and unsheathe my claws.
Reality's worth defending.

*Snake blaming:*
Don't tell me a snake was evil for suggesting I grow.
That snake is God's creature, just like I am.
Don't tell me the truth can't come
from someone who changes—
that just makes me examine
more carefully the skins she shed
because anything, or anyone, who grows
so full of knowing she has to ditch the past,

that's something, or someone, I need to know.

*Mary and Martha:*
You know, Jesus never told women
to get back in the kitchen
because it was a sin for women
to belly up to Christ's table.
He was a teacher so learning
and knowing was what he was all about.
So he told Martha to buzz off
when she wanted Mary to quit
talking and start peeling potatoes,
and he sat Mary down with the men.
like she was every bit as important.
I take that as a personal invitation
because I share her name.
It's no sin to know, no sin to explore,
no sin to reach for the truth,
no sin to question—
that's not God talking
that's some alternative-fact demon
spinning tales.

*10 Commandments:*
When some thug rapes you, lies to you,
manipulates you, steals from you, and stunned
by the wickedness, you are silent
there is no sin to that at 14,
but if you are still silent at 20 or 30 or 40,
you betray yourself and all the children of God
by kneeling to some false prophet.
Yell the truth,
stare down evil through your tears,
hold a press conference,
write it in cement, and tell the world:
"You fuckers aren't running the show anymore!"

And then set that stone next to the Ten Commandments
on some Alabama courthouse lawn.
People need reminding by something—
by someone—immutable and knowing.
Knowledge gives you the power,
to shed your fears and right wrongs.
Be Eve.
Bite the apple.

## Ghostwritten

She sometimes was so quiet
the chipmunks by the river,
where she spread her blanket,
scampered and played as if she weren't there.
She often wasn't.
She was somewhere in her head
writing stories of people she met—
ghostwriting their lives in playlets
and dramas she kept inside,
so she felt then that she knew them—
knew how they felt,
how they breathed,
how they spent a Saturday night,
what they drank with dinner,
how they spoke to lovers and children.

Sometimes the people outside her head
veered off script in ways she hadn't imagined.
And when they did
she went back down to the river,
or walked along the bike path near it,
and cleared her head and rewrote
the stories she kept within.

And the longer she took things in,
the more she revised,
the less their stories mattered.
One day she stopped trying
to encase people in words
and freed them to their own devices,
and she left the river
and the chipmunks
and found another path
where she breathed in her own story
unghosted.

## Divorce Decree:  Untethered


Now that you are gone, I remember the ropes
that drew me back when I wanted to soar.
Loosed, I am sky-driven, delighted in my wing span,
captivated by the shadow I throw to earth.

I cannot say I miss my ropes,
though I sometimes long for connections.
Still, the air, clear blue
or sweet with rain—
or even rigid with frosted clouds—
draws me more tightly
than the steel bands
once binding me to my lover's breast.

And so I rise shedding regrets, arching skyward
breathing free—untethered.

## Reflective Reading

A line curves my cheek,
a surgical scar now pseudo-wrinkle,
testament to my doctor's skill
removing cancer from my face.
His worth exceeded his blades
when his kindness made
me feel the worth of who I am.

Between my eyes two vertical lines—
a teacher once told me,
to my delight,
they would become permanent,
"if I didn't stop frowning."
I liked the hawkish look
and so I use them to mark concentration,
puzzlement, anger, regrets.

My nose crooks like my grandfather's.
I smile at it.  He protected me all my life
from the curse of beauty—
that vapid blankness
in which some read their desires
then forget the real person within.
I've always known I was loved.

Cataracts gone, my eyes shine true blue.
The smokiness hazed the windows to my core,
 but youth returns—Psyche never ages.

In the tangle of the morning light,
my hair more gray than blond now
shimmers back at me
in bounces, waves.
I've let it grow longer
and carry my past
on its strands.

**Love Letters**

I do not write love letters
on scented paper to enfold
in crinkly envelopes.
No, moonlit night or sunlit day
inspires me to imprint my love
on sugar-sanded beaches.
I've never scrawled my heart's desires
on postcards from any edge.
No selfie tagged with smiling face
signals my love; instead,
I wear my love like a second skin
encasing all I do,
and if you cannot read it in my pose,
trace my scars
and read closer for what is true.

**Unfinished Story**

Sometimes grief darts before me,
on paths I would otherwise ignore.
It whispers directions on an errant breeze,
points the way to something buried.
When I'm lost, it speaks silence,
no happy echo of the past.
It lies unanswered like my prayers,
hollow and unholy.
Sometimes it seeps inside, empties my heart
then fills it with rush of memory—
a crushing hunger,
for something lost, unfulfilled
half-done.

## Lip-read

I remember your pretty pout
as you considered your bike's gears.
I watched as your lips compressed in concentration.
Then your mouth went crooked.
You turned the pedals so you could shift
the gears up and down chains.
Your lips moved with each clicking transitions.
The briefest smile crossed your mouth in satisfaction,
as your hand reached for an oil can
to soothe clinking wheels
and your lips went silent.

## In Memoriam: Christmas Greetings

Suspended in the space outside a snow-framed window,
grief floats above the sandy snowscape to comfort me.
On my couch, trapped in the gravity of loss, I flip
calendar pages that once again counted down
another year without you.

Again, we will not share the lights of our Christmas tree
nor sample cookies I bake for Christmas Day.
I won't catch you stealing deviled eggs
from the trays I plan to take to parties.
And I know, even if that is all I'd want for Christmas,
I cannot bring you back

So as you funnel down to that emptiness above the snow
and evaporate into the stars, look my way as you go.
Feel the pull of my love suspended in that inaccessible blankness
where once we touched, where I still embrace
what bridged us, and in the brightness of that light
wish me "Merry Christmas" once again.

## Empty Air:  Epitaph

When the air empties of you,
and I no longer find your scent
in the flannel of your coat
hanging still in the garage;
when the shape of the trees you planted shifts
and I replace the coneflowers
withering without your touch;
when I rearrange the furniture
so I no longer look for you in your chair—
when I no longer cry when I open your drawers
to find socks neatly paired as you left them—
the ache of your absence will still throb in my bones,
as I look off the deck remembering
the shape of you in moonlight.

**M**ary Fox is a Michigan-born poet, currently residing in Portland, MI. She graduated from Michigan State University (BA) and Central Michigan University (MS). Prior to retirement, she worked primarily as a full-time Fowler High School teacher. During this time, she also taught part-time for Lansing Community College. At Fowler, she served not only as a teacher but also as the union president and its chief negotiator, a coach for basketball and softball, a play director, a class sponsor, and many other roles, including producing yearly publications of student writing. When she retired in 2010, she began working in earnest on her own writing.

In 2016, she published *Waiting for Rain*, a poetry chapbook, with Finishing Line Press, and in 2018 co-edited and contributed to a Writing-at-the-Ledges fourth anthology, *Promptly Speaking*, for her writing group. Currently, in addition to working with two writing groups, she volunteers with Lansing Poetry Club.

Last year, Finishing Line Press afforded Mary Fox, Alan Harris (*Hospice Bed Conversations* and *Fall Ball, poetry for the late innings*) and Rosalie Sanara Petrouske (*A Postcard From My Mother* and *What We Keep*) the opportunity to choose and mentor a new poet to publication. Finishing Line has now made the contest a yearly opportunity with the Lansing Poetry Club, and the contest is known as the Ritzenhein Emerging Poet Award. Mary currently serves as its coordinator.

Mary Fox continues to read poetry, conduct workshops, and engage with other poets in the Lansing area. Her favorite venue is the Robin Theatre in Reo Town, a section of Lansing, Michigan. Outside of poetry, mentoring, other writing, and editing, Mary enjoys friends, family, travel, golf, swimming, plays, musical performances, and a cat named Boguy.

www.ingramcontent.com/pod-product-compliance
Lightning Source LLC
LaVergne TN
LVHW041508070426
835507LV00012B/1404